The Rhythm Lab's Traditional Drum Set Classic Grooves & Fills

For Recitals

Contemporary Studies for Traditional Drum Set

By Bermudian Author and Professor

Eddie Ming

Second Edition

ISBN Number: 978-0-9569878-0-8

Published by: Eddie Ming Publishing
Mailing address of the publisher:
Eddie Ming's Rhythm Lab, # 9 – 39 Cut Road, St. George's GE 04, B E R M U D A
Fax: 441-297-4361
E-mail: emingflatride@btcnet.bm
Or, eddiemingflatride@gmail.com

Printed by CreateSpace

Available from Amazon.com
&
The Rhythm Lab – BERMUDA
&
Eddie Ming's Drum School, Bermuda

El Laboratorio del Ritmo Grooves De Batería Tradicional Clásico y Rellenos para Recitales

Estudios Contemporáneos
por El Grupo de Percusión Tradicional

Por el autor y professor de Las Bermudas

Eddie Ming

Segunda Edición

Número de ISBN: 978-0-9569878-0-8

Publicado por La Editorial Eddie Ming
Dirección de envoi del editor:
Eddie Ming's Rhythm Lab, # 9 – 39 Cut Road, St. George's GE 04, Las BERMUDAS
Fax: 441-297-4361
Dirección por correo electrónico:
emingflatride@btcnet.bm o, eddiemingflatride@gmail.com

Impreso por CreateSpace

Disponible en Amazon.com
y
El Laboratorio Del Ritmo – Las BERMUDAS
y
La Escuela de Batería de Eddie Ming, Las Bermudas

Contents

Índice

26 Grooves Clásicos

10 Grooves Dedicados

ABOUT THE AUTHOR ERNEST EDWARD MING

Eddie Ming was born in the parish of Devonshire, Bermuda, and now resides in the parish of St. George's with his wife, Wendy Rosemarie.

Eddie emerged on the Bermuda music scene in the mid 1960's, and was recognized for his phenomenal reading skills. He replaced his former teacher from Boston, Massacheusetts, Bill Joyce, at 'The Carlton Beach Hotel' in Southampton, Bermuda, where he became the resident show drummer with ' The Ruby Newman Boston Society Orchestra'. He continued to work there full time for five years. After five years, he felt that it was time to move on, so he applied to the resident band at 'The Castle Harbour Hotel', where he became the resident drummer for ' The Castle Harbour Hotel Society Orchestra', while studying with Bermuda's legendary Jazz drummer, Clarence 'Tootsie' Bean. While he was studying with 'Tootsie,' Eddie also studied with the late Ghandi Burgess's drummer and Jazz promoter, Charles Bascome, who at that time was recognized for teaching George Stone's Stick Control Method. Eddie also studied with Joe Wiley and The Hamilton Princess Hotel Orchestra's English Jazz drummer and composer, Alan Ganley, for two years. When 'Tootsie' decided to move to New York, he asked Eddie to replace him at 'The Inverurie Hotel', where Eddie worked for the next fourteen years, with musical director, Johnny McAteer. After leaving the McAteer 'gig', he went on to study at New York City's premier music school : ' The Collective,' where he graduated. While he was at 'The Collective,' he studied with John Coltrane's former drummer, Rashia Alie. In Cuba, he studied with Enrique Pla and Jose Luis Quintana "Changuito." He is currently studying at New York's Conservatory For The Performing Arts.

For the past thirty-five years, Eddie has developed and taught a program which is dedicated to nurturing the art of drumming in young children. In 1977, Eddie produced and sponsored Bermuda's First International Jazz and Drum Clinic, featuring United States Jazz drummer. Freddie Waits, followed by other renowned US percussionists, Harvey Mason and Charlie Persip. Eddie is founder and director of 'The Rhythm Lab,' which introduces his students to many music and percussion programs outside of Bermuda.

Eddie teaches annually at the Escuela Elemental de Música 'Alejandro Garcia Caturla,' in Havana, Cuba, for three weeks of the year, and in 2009, the school presented him with a Teacher's Diploma ' for his valuable contribution to the Methodology of teaching Percussion.'

Eddie is very grateful that he was recognized by the Bermuda Arts Council, and that he was a recipient of a Badge of Honour from Her Majesty, Queen Elizabeth II of England.

Up until today, Eddie is still Bermuda's most sought after drum teacher, who comes with a wealth of knowledge, and the ability to teach at all levels.

SOBRE EL AUTOR ERNEST EDWARD MING

Eddie Ming nació en la parroquia de Devonshire, en las Bermudas, y ahora reside en la parroquia de San George con su mujer, Wendy Rosemarie.

Eddie brotó en la escena musical de las Bermudas a mediados de 1960; y fue reconocido por sus habilidades fenomenales de lectura. Reemplazó a su maestro anterior de Boston, Massacheusetts, Bill Joyce, en 'El Hotel de Playa de Carlton' en Southampton, en las Bermudas, donde llegó a ser el tambor morador de exposición con 'La Ruby Newman Boston Sociedad Orquesta.' Continuó a trabajar a tiempo completo durante cinco años. Después de cinco años, él sentía que era tiempo de seguir adelante, así que aplicó a la banda residente en 'El Hotel de Puerto de Castillo,' donde llegó a ser el tambor natural de 'La Orquesta de la Sociedad del Hotel de Puerto de Castillo,' al estudiar con tambor legendario de Jazz de las Bermudas, Clarence "Tootsie" Bean. Mientras estudiaba con "Tootsie," Eddie también estudió con el tambor del tarde Diputado de Ghandi, y promoter de Jazz, Charles Bascome, que fue reconocido en aquel momento por enseñar el Método del Control del Palo de George Stone. Eddie también estudió con Joe Wiley y El Tambor inglés de Jazz de Orquesta de Hotel de Princesa de Hamilton y con el compositor, Alan Ganley, durante dos años. Cuando "Tootsie" decidió mudarse a Nueva York, él pidió que Eddie de reemplazarlo en 'El Hotel de Inverurie,' donde Eddie trabajó durante los próximos catorce años, con el director musical, Johnny McAteer. Después de dejar la "actuación" de McAteer, él pasó a estudiar en la escuela primera de música de Ciudad de Nueva York : 'El Colectivo,' donde él se graduó. Mientras estuvo en 'El Colectivo,' estudió con tamborista anterior de John Coltrane, Rashia Alie. En Cuba, él estudió con Enrique Plá y José Luis Quintana "Changuito." Eddie enseña anualmente en la Escuela Elemental de Música 'Alejandro García Caturla,' tres semanas por año, y en 2009, fue presentado con el Diploma de Maestro. Estudia actualmente en el Conservatorio de Nueva York Para Las Artes Interpretativas.

Durante los últimos treinta y cinco años, Eddie ha desarrollado y ha enseñado un programa que es dedicado al arte de tocar el tambor en niños jóvenes. En 1977, Eddie produjo y patrocinó la primera clinica de Jazz Internacional de Bermuda y Dispensario de Batería, representando a tambor de Jazz de EEUU, Freddie Waits, seguido por otros percusionistas renombrados de EEUU, Harvey Mason y Charlie Persip.

Eddie es fundador y director del 'Laboratorio de Ritmo,' que introduce a sus estudiantes a muchas músicas y al programa de percussion fuera de las Bermudas.

En 2009, fue concedido Eddie un Diploma por la Escuela Elemental de Música 'Alejandro García Caturla,' en la Habana, Cuba, para su contribución valiosa a la Metodología de Baterías y Percusión docentes.'

Eddie está muy agradecido que fue reconocido por la Asamblea de Artes de las Bermudas, y recibió la Insignia de Honor de Su Majestad, la Reina Elizabeth II de Inglaterra.

Hasta el dia de hoy, Eddie es el maestro de batería mas amble de las Bermudas, que viene con el conocimiento en abundancia, y la capacidad de enseñar a cada nivel.

CNEArt

THE NATIONAL CENTER OF ARTS SCHOOLS OF CUBA awards the present acknowledgement to:

ERNEST EDWARD MING, professor of percussion from Bermudas for:

His valuable contribution to the Methodology of teaching Traditional Drums at the Conservatory "Amadeo Roldán" in May 2008

So that this may be officially recorded and in witness whereof, the undersigned hereto set their hand in Havana, Cuba on the eighteenth day of December, 2010

Rolando Ortega Álvarez
Director

CNEArt

THE NATIONAL CENTER OF ARTS SCHOOLS OF CUBA awards the present acknowledgement to:

ERNEST EDWARD MING, professor of percussion from Bermudas for:

His valuable contribution to the Methodology of teaching Traditional Drums at CNARI, in December 2010

So that this may be officially recorded and in witness whereof, the undersigned hereto set their hand in Havana, Cuba on the eighteenth day of December, 2010

Rolando Ortega Alvarez
Director

THE NATIONAL CENTER OF ARTS SCHOOLS OF
CUBA awards the present acknowledgement to:

ERNEST EDWARD MING, professor of percussion
from Bermudas for:

Creating a Cultural Exchange Program between the Escuela
Nacional de Música de Cuba and Eddie Ming's Rhythm Lab,
Bermuda in 2008

So that this may be officially recorded and in witness
whereof, the undersigned hereto set their hand in Havana,
Cuba on the eighteenth day of December, 2010

Rolando Ortega Álvarez
Director

THE NATIONAL CENTER OF ARTS SCHOOLS OF CUBA awards the present acknowledgement to:

ERNEST EDWARD MING, professor of percussion from Bermudas for:

His valuable contribution to the Methodology of teaching Traditional Drums at the Elementary Music School " Alejandro García Caturla," in 2009

So that this may be officially recorded and in witness whereof, the undersigned hereto set their hand in Havana, Cuba on the eighteenth day of December, 2010

Rolando Ortega Álvarez
Director

In the name of

Her Majesty
Queen Elizabeth the Second

This Certificate of Honour
is awarded to

Professor Eddie Ming

of _St. George's Parish_

in recognition of valuable services given to Her Majesty

for his service to the world of music

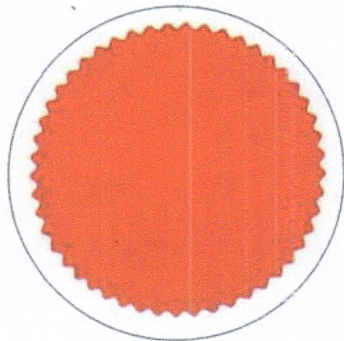

Date _31st December 2008_

Richard Gozney

Governor and Commander-in-Chief

9

ABOUT 120 KIDS rocked to the beat of a different drum when Mr. Eddy Ming conducted a lecture-demonstration on the principles of music at Warwick Secondary as part of the Government sponsored summer day camps. Some of Mr. Ming's students participated as well, helping their mates to appreciate the music.

NJOYING THE "BEAUTIFUL EX-ERIENCE", Mr. Eddy Ming drums up a orm for the youngsters at the summer day imp music expo. The kids, aged from five to ven, asked Mr. Ming back to continue the brations which Mr. Ming says come natu-lly to children.

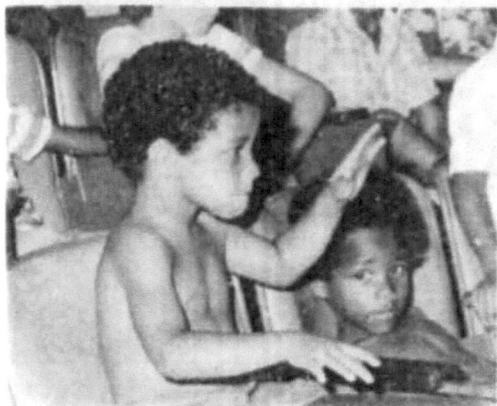

THIS YOUNGSTER is obviously enjoying himself as he rocks to the vibrations which Mr. Ming says are children's natural gift, and a valuable teaching aid, as it makes them so easy to work with.

Review

by

Cuban Lecturer and Teacher of English and Spanish

Prof. Sonia Salas

December 20, 2009

The wait of several months ended with the arrival of Professor Ming in Havana. All students and teachers of percussion at the Caturla School of Music were eager to begin the much talked about Percussion Workshop, and for that Ming was there.

He organized small workshops according to grade levels, and taught for two weeks. The working sessions were fruitful, and everyone enjoyed the individual and group practices.

The final activity - a recital - was held at 'Plaza's Casa de La Cultura', a popular place for performances by famous artists. Soon, the building was packed with students and parents and teachers. The boys put into practice all the experience passed on to them by Professor Ming, and even shared the stage with musicians from other schools and of different levels.

December 2009, is now in the memory of all Caturla Music School's percussionists, together with the idea of welcoming back Professor Ming again, for more.

Examen

por

Profesor cubano y profesor de inglés y español

Profesor Sonia Salas

20 de diciembre 2009

La espera de varios meses terminaba con la llegada del profesor Ming a La Habana. Todos los estudiantes y profesores de percusión de la escuela de música Caturla estaban ansiosos por comenzar el tan comentado Taller de Percusión y para eso Ming estaba allí.

El organizó pequeños talleres de acuerdo a los grados escolares e impartió clases durante dos semanas. Las sesiones de trabajo fueron fructíferas donde todos disfrutaron la práctica individual y en grupos.

La actividad final se celebró en La Casa de La Cultura de Plaza, conocido lugar por las actuaciones de artistas famosos. Muy pronto el local estaba lleno de estudiantes y padres. Los muchachos pusieron en práctica toda la experiencia legada por el professor Ming, e incluso compartieron el escenario con músicos de otras escuelas y niveles.

Diciembre de 2009 queda hoy en el recuerdo de todos los percusionistas de la escuela Caturla unido a la idea de recibir nuevamente al profesor Ming.

KOSA

Friday, July 9th 2010

Montreal's

KoSa Centre des Arts

proudly presents

Prof. Eddie Ming's Percussion Trio

BOJO

With special guests,

Bryson Doers & Tajai O'Connor

Theme entitled : CALCULATIONS

Theme Description :

Blending Dominican rhythms with Funk,

to create new ideas

that reflect strength and enthusiasm.

KOSA

viernes, 9 de Julio del 2010

El centro de artes KoSa de Montreal

presenta

El trío percusionista del Prof. Eddie Ming

"BOJO"

Con invitados especiales

Bryson Doers y Tajai O'Connor

Tema: Cálculos

Objetivo:

Mezclar los ritmos Dominicanos con la música de tipo Funk

para crear nuevas ideas

que reflejan fuerza y pasión.

PREFACE

The main objective of this text is to help in building a solid foundation of understanding, so that these Classic Grooves may be executed with little difficulty. In addition to being stimulating to all drum students at 'Caturla,' it will help them to broaden their scope.

CLASSIC GROOVE NOTES

All new styles need to be nurtured by daily repetition and patience; and by the student staying motivated. The real object, is for you to play these grooves musically.

Use a metronome when practising these grooves.

Each student is responsible for his or her own Starting Tempo. The tempos that are indicated are just suggestions.

Bass or Kick Drum : All rhythms should be executed with the pureness of deep and soulful sound that comes from one's heart.

Hi-Hat or Sock Cymbal : The sound and motion of the Hi-Hat rhythms must continue to labour and produce regular activity and quality time.

Snare Drum : All snare drum accents should be played as rim shots with good balance, and a great announcement of authority.

Play each groove for 10 minutes or more each day without stopping, and without fills, until each groove feels good, and then play as written, with a 1 bar fill, and so on.

You may want to verify these grooves by listening to famous recording artists such as: Keith Sweat, Martell Jordan, Kelly Price, Teddy Pendergrass, Gerald Levert; and session greats such as Bernard ('Pretty') Purdie, who was featured in Eddie Ming's Annual Drum Exhibition at his Bermuda Drum School in 1978.

The proceeding page features a photo of Bernard ('Pretty') Purdie, and an interview with him.

PREFACIO

El objetivo principal de este texto es contribuir en la construcción de una base sólida de entendimiento, de modo que estos "grooves' clásicos pueden ser ejecutado con poca dificultad. Además de ser estimulante para todos los estudiantes de tambor 'Caturla,' que les ayudará a ampliar su ámbito de aplicación.

NOTAS CLÁSICOS DE "GROOVE"

Todos los nuevos estilos necesidad de ser alimentado por la repetición diaria y paciencia, y por el estudiante permanecer motivado. El objeto real, es para que usted juegue estos 'grooves' musicalmente.

Utilice un metrónomo en la prática de estos 'grooves.'

Cada estudiante es responsable de su propio partir Tempo. Los tiempos que se indican son solo sugerencias.

Bombo : Todos los ritmos se debe ejecutar con la pureza de alma profunda y de sonido que viene del corazón de uno.

Hi-Hat (platillos cerrados) : El sonido y el movimiento de los ritmos Hi-Hat debe continuar con el trabajo y producir actividad regular y tiempo de calidad.

Caja : Todos los acentos de caja se deben jugar como golpes de aro con buen equilibrio y un gran anuncio de la autoridad.

Escuchar cada 'groove' una durante de 10 minutos o más. cada día sin parar, y sin rellenos, hasta que cada groove se siente bien, y luego jugar como por escrito, con un relleno de un bar, y así sucesivamente.

Es possible que desee comprobar estos grooves por escuchar a los artistas más famosos, como Keith Sweat, Jordan Martell, Kelly Price, Teddy Pendergrass, Gerald Levert, y los grandes de la session, como Bernard ('Pretty') Purdie, que fue ofrecido en Eddie's Exposición Annual del Tambor de su escuela del tambor de las Bermudas en 1978.

La página de procedimiento ofrece una foto de Bernard ('Pretty') Purdie, y una entrevista con él.

Master drummer, Eddie Ming, the man who has probably done more than any other single musician in Bermuda to teach his art to others, presents his second annual exhibition and drumming clinic on May 7.

Last year, with guest lecturer Freddie Waits from the United States, the show was a runaway success, and this time, with guest percussionist Bernard (Pretty) Purdie conducting, the formula is as before. With one big difference, and that is the opportunity of Eddie Ming's students to show how much extra skill they have attained in the past 12 months.

The exhibition and clinic is at the Galaxy Nightclub, starting at 6 p.m. M.C. is Earl Williams and trophies will be presented by Viola Ming.

Apart from performances by students, Eddie's percussion group "Storm" will be back with solo artists Sandra Simmons and ' The Pack,' dancing star Michael Ebbin, and Ronnie Lopes, Winston Lightbourn and Kenny Ebbin.

Also on the programme are Eddie's Jazz Sextet, featuring Mr. Upright Henry Jones, and a Transcendental Meditation lecture by Stuart Hayward.

Bernard Purdie got his nickname 'Pretty' from the "mighty pretty" way he plays the drums. Born in Elton, Maryland, U.S.A., he has been drumming for more than 30 years, and now has about 125 students.

Purdie has recorded with just about everybody, from advertising agencies cutting television commercials to some of the top recording stars in the business. A university in North Carolina conducted a survey in 1975 on recordings and found that he has recorded more than 3,000 albums!

He is currently playing with ' Hummingbird' – Diamond Nights' Band which was born in 1972 after Jeff Beck's 'Rough and Ready' group disbanded. He has worked on movie soundtracks, including 'Hair' and – coming out in December – 'Sergeant Pepper's Lonely Hearts Club Band,' and done television soundtracks including 'Dear Daughter and Quincy.'

Eddie Ming said: "Last year I decided that as a teacher and drummer with so many students who have great potential, I would produce and present a drumming exhibition and clinic that would give them something to go after – and at the same time, change the standard of drumming in this country.'

' The show did just what I hoped it would do. Not only has it inspired all my students, but the exposure has done them a whole lot of good. It has put them on a higher level.'

' Take 14 year old Tyrone Bean, for instance. The clinic and exhibition inspired him so much that in less than 12 months he has gone from being unable to play a drum set at all, to being able to really prove what it takes. Charlie Franks, another newcomer to my school is the most natural drummer I have heard for some time. His conception and creativity never ceases to surprise me.'

Another newcomer to the Ming School is George Simmons, well known for his dynamic singing with ' Formula of Love.' He is devoted to study; and because of his discipline, Eddie is confident he will become one of Bermuda's outstanding show drummers.

Also, at this year's show, will again be Bermuda's female drumming star-in-the-making, Kim Smith, and the phenomenal 12-year old Antoine Jones.

'The Royal Gazette,' Bermuda, 1979

Notation Key
Clave de la Notación

Closed Hi-hat
Hi-hat cerrado

Open Hi-hat
Hi-hat abierto

Hi-hat opened and closed w/foot
Hi-hat abierto y cerrado con el pie

Ride cymbal
Platillo ride

Crash cymbal
Platillo crash

Bass Drum
Bombo

Snare
Caja

Tom 1
Tom tom de aire

Tom 2
Tom tom de aire 2

Tom 3
Tom tom de piso

Cymbal Bell
Copa del platillo

Stick on stick
Baqueta sobre baqueta

*U = unison sticking
*U = golpear con las dos baquetas al unisono

16

Presented here, is a list of terms used in this text:

REPEAT SIGNS
Play the measure within the repeat signs

REPEAT MEASURE SIGN
Repeat the preceding measure

REPEAT MEASURE SIGN
Repeat the number of preceding measures indicated

CONTINUE TO KEEP THE TIME GOING

ACCENTED NOTE

ABBREVIATIONS/SYMBOLS:

CB = CYMBAL BELL

SD = SNARE DRUM

RC = RIDE CYMBAL

FT = FLOOR TOM

HH = HI-HAT

BD = BASS DRUM

TT = TOM TOM

"Fingering" in connection with drumming, refers to the Right and Left Hand
strokes, such as R R L L, R L R R, etc.

Se presenta aquí una lista de términos utilizados en este texto:

LOS SIGNOS DE REPETICIÓN
Tocar los compases dentro de los signos de repetición

EL SIGNO DE REPETICIÓN
Repita el compás anterior

EL SIGNO DE REPETICIÓN
Repita el número indicado de compases anteriores

SIGA MANTENIENDO EL TIEMPO

UNA NOTA ACENTUADA

ABREVIATURAS/SÍMBOLOS:

CB = LA COPA DE PLATILLO   *SD = CAJA*

RC = PLATILLO "RIDE"   *FD = TOM TOM DE PIE*

HH = PLATILLOS CERRADO (HI-HAT)   *BD = BOMBO*

TT = TOM TOM DE AIRE

"Dedos" en relación con tambores, se refiere a la derecha y golpes de la mano izquierda como D D I I, D I D D, etc.

GROOVE EXECUTION

In order to get a better understanding of each groove in this text, I would suggest that you use the A,B,C, and D examples.

Example A : Practice bass and snare only.

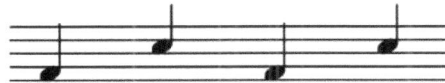

Example B : Hi-Hat and bass drum only.

Example C : Hi-Hat and snare drum only.

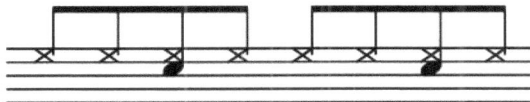

Example D : Played in unison - Bass drum on 1 and 3, snare drum 2 and 4, with straight eighth on Hi-Hat.

NOTE: The same principle applies for quarter notes and sixteenth notes Hi-Hat patterns with alternating bass drum and snare drum beats.

Through the use of this procedure, you will find that you will get remarkable results.

EJECUCIÓN DEL GROOVE

Con el fin de conseguir una mejor comprensión de cada groove en este texto, le sugiero que utilice la A, ejemplos B, C y D.

Ejemplo A : El bombo y caja solamente.

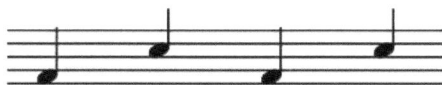

Ejemplo B : Hi-Hat y el bombo solamente.

Ejemplo C: Hi-Hat y caja solamente

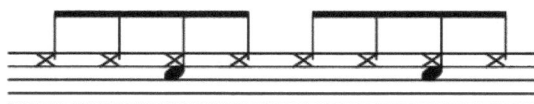

Ejemplo D: Jugado al unísono - Bombo en el 1 y en el 3, caja en el 2 y en el 4 con corchea consecutiva en Hi-Hat.

NOTA: El mismo principio se aplica para las negras y semicorcheas Hi-Hat patrones con alternancia de bombo y caja.

A través del uso de este procedimiento, usted encontrará que usted conseguirá resultados notables.

Malecón Funk

Meet me at Caturla

♩=60

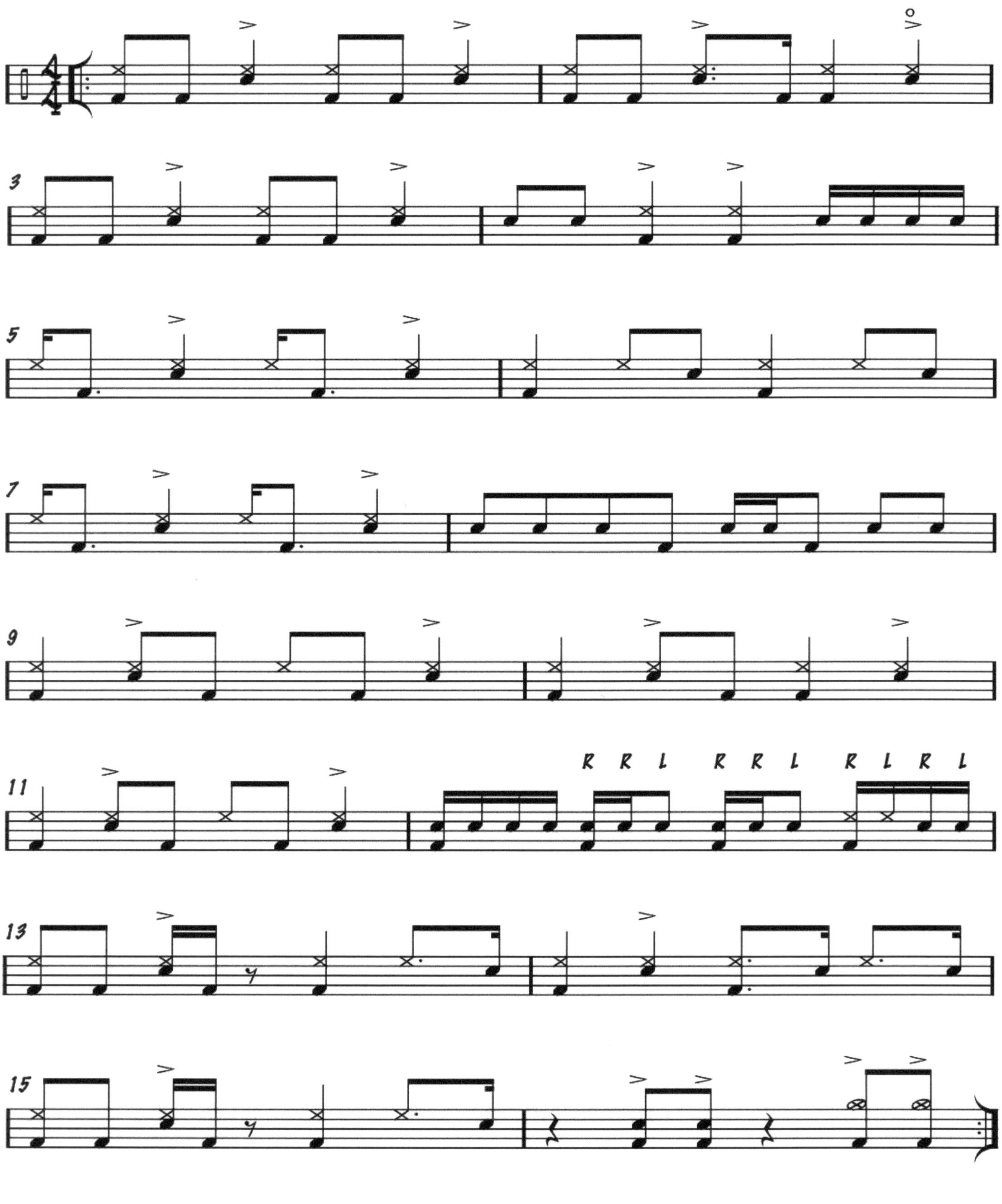

My Casa

♩=60

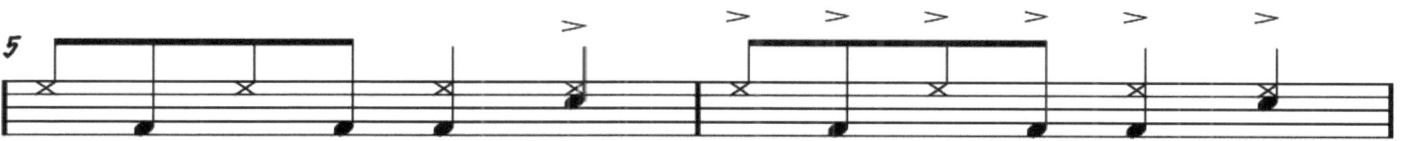

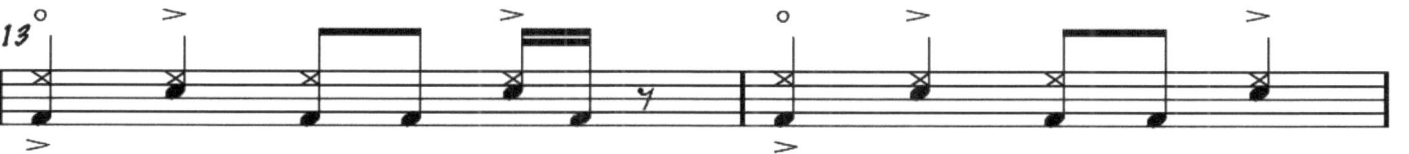

Havana Love

♩=60

Pigeon Square

Classic Grooves #1

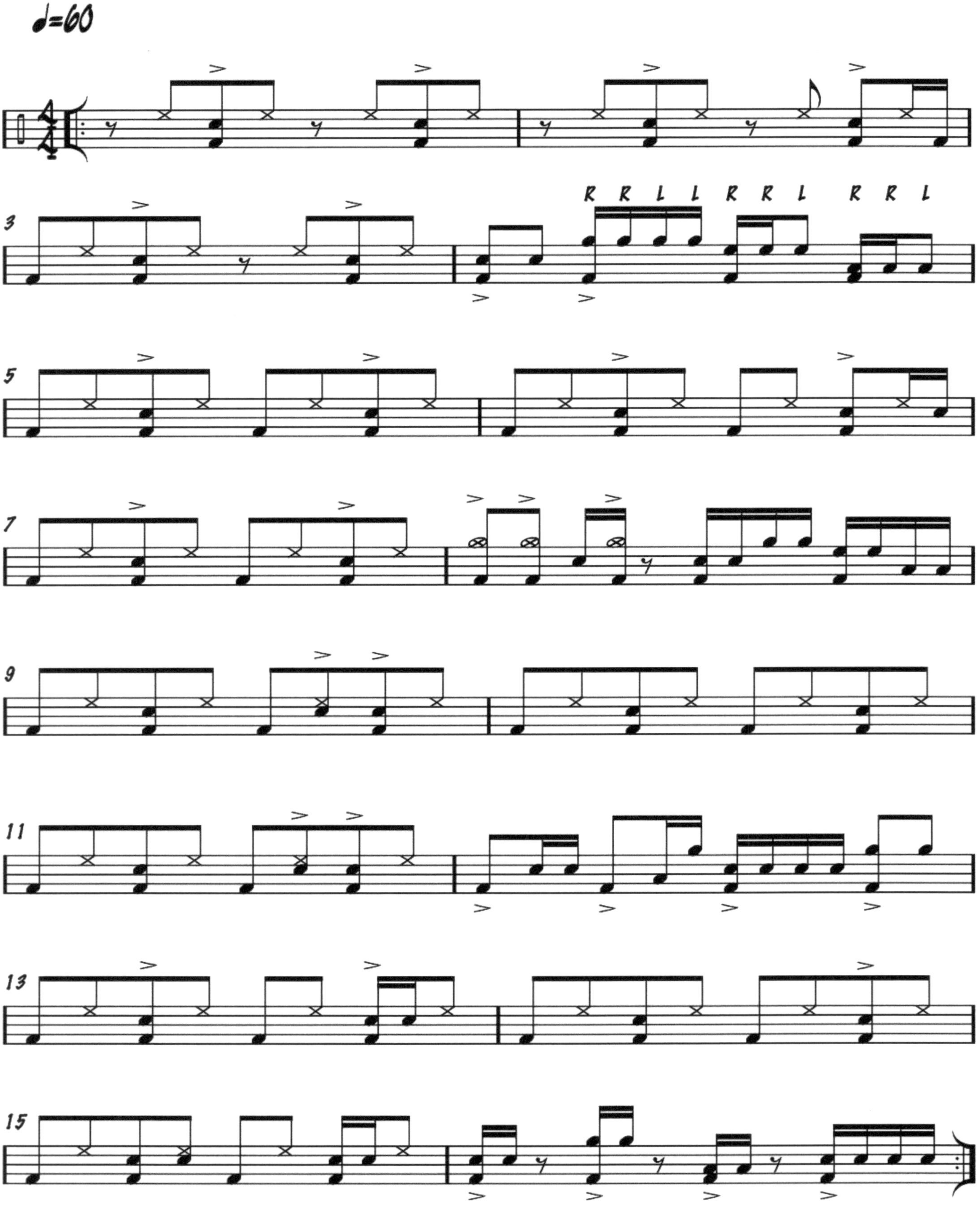

I Found Cuba

Classic Grooves #2

Coco Taxi

Classic Grooves #3

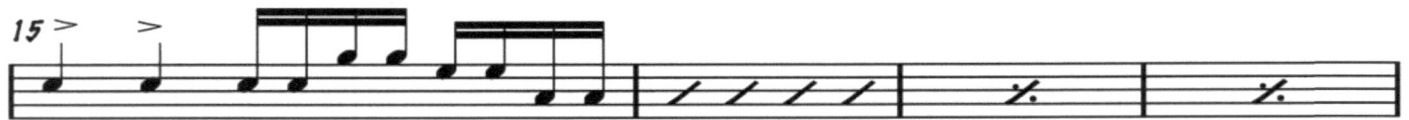

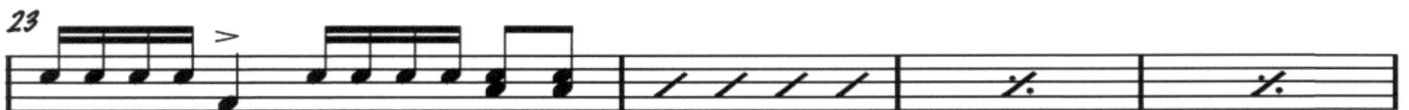

Classic Grooves #4

♩=60

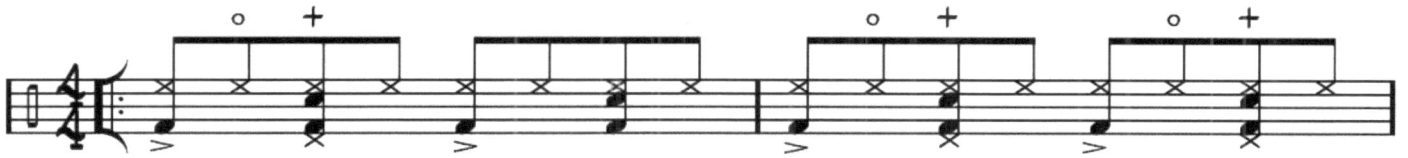

Classic Grooves #5

Classic Grooves #6

♩=60

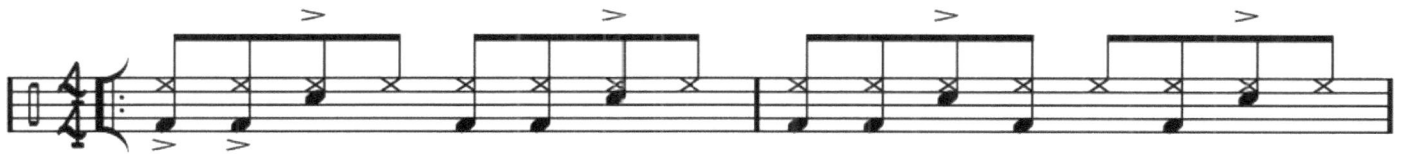

Fruiterer

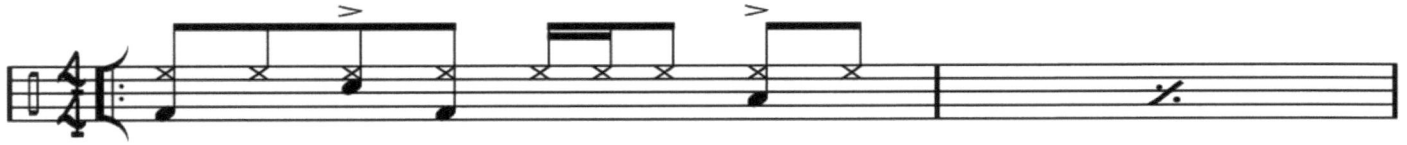

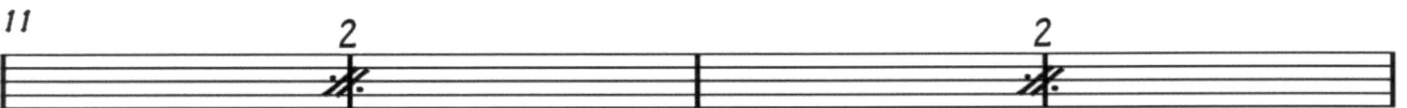

Children of Caturla

Somewhere in Playa

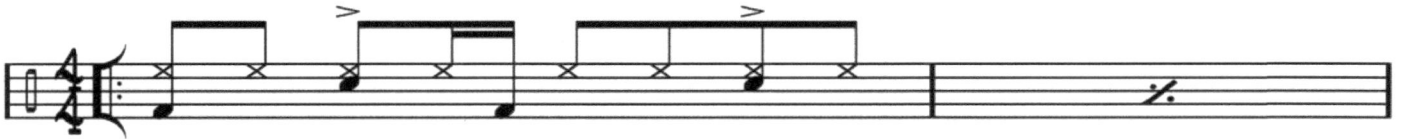

Just 50-Cuc

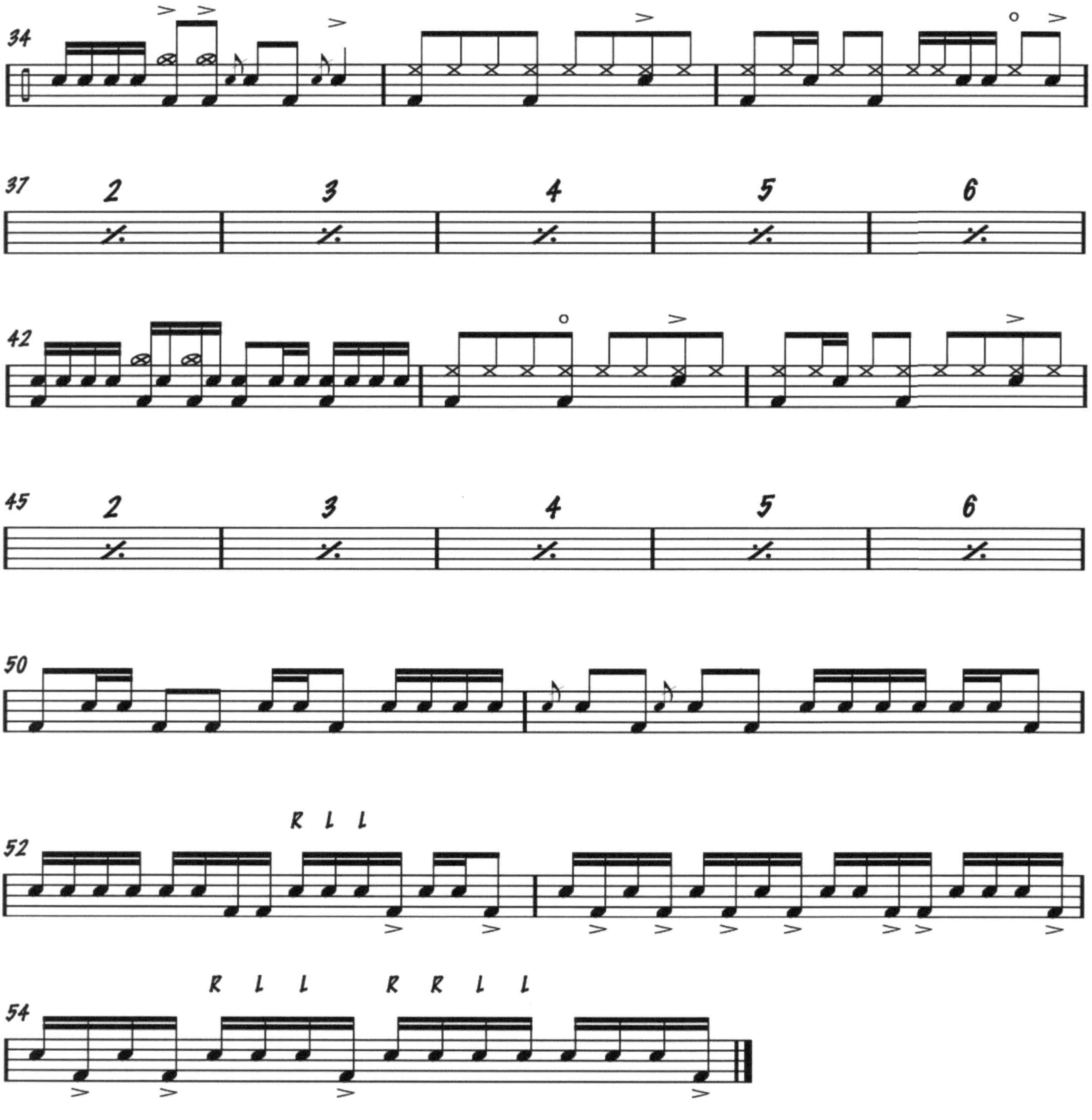
34
37
2
3
4
5
6
42
45
2
3
4
5
6
50
R L L
52
R L L R R L L
54

Classic Grooves #7

TV 9

Classic Grooves #8

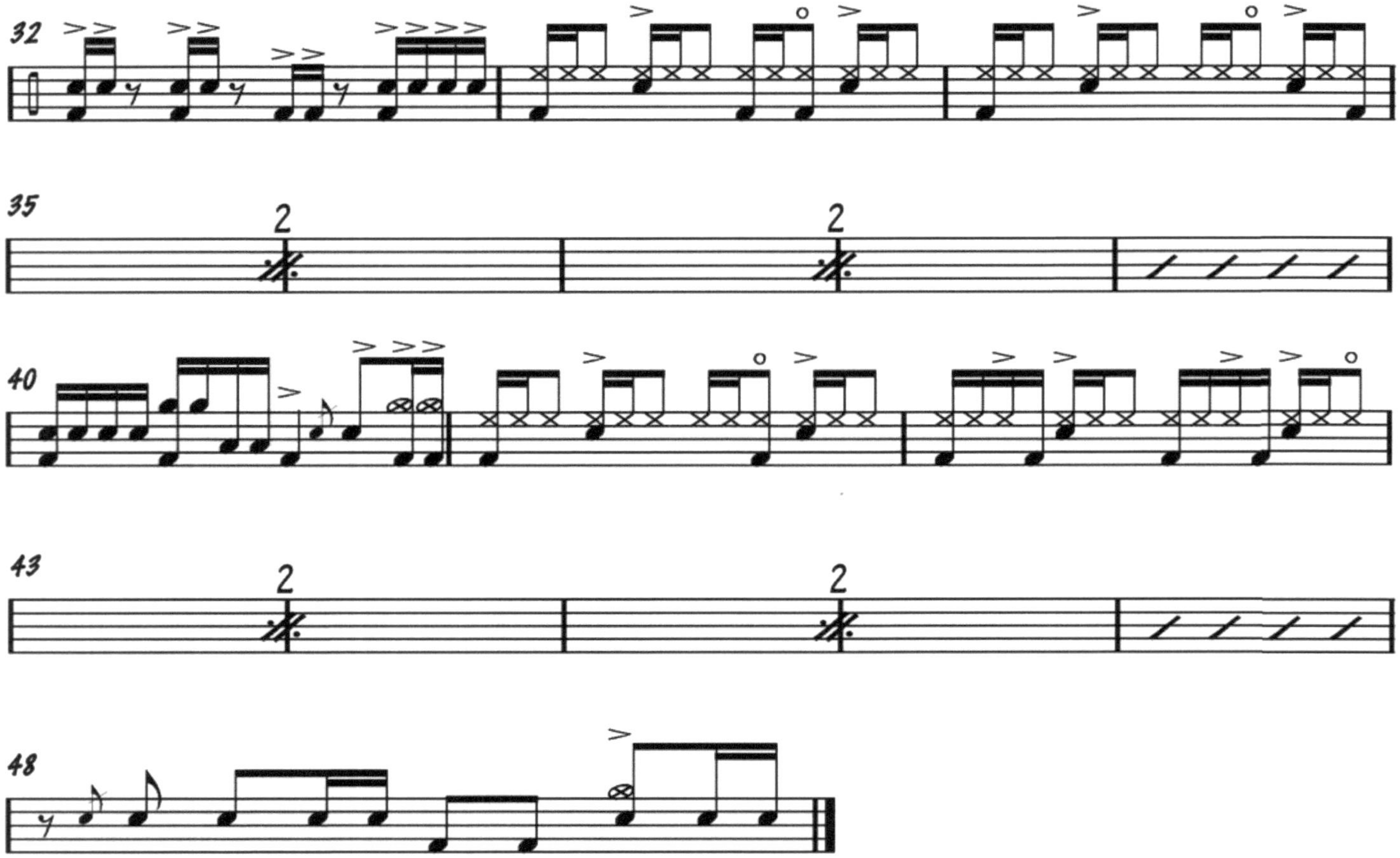
32
35
2
2
40
43
2
2
48

Classic Grooves #9

Classic Grooves #10

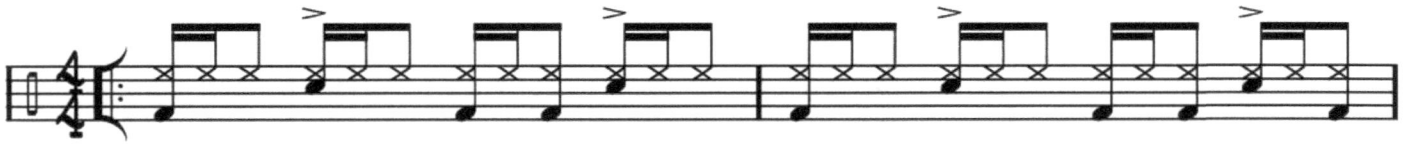

Classic Grooves #11

Classic Grooves #12

Classic Grooves #13

Garcia, Garcia

Escuela Elemental de Musica
Alejandro Garcia Caturla
Presenta la introduccion a

L'ESPRIT DE CORPS

I II III

Conducido por
el profesor bermudense

EDDIE MING

Apoyado por

SABIAN CYMBAL MAKERS

De New Brunswick, Canada.

Fecha: **Viernes**, Diciembre 3, 2009
Lugar: Escuela A. GARCIA CATURLA
Hora: 10.00a.m. a 12.00p.m.
Para mas information por favor llamar
a la Escuela CATURLA
Telef. 260-4525

Patrocinado por

SABIAN, RHYTHM LAB DE BERMUDA Y
EL MEMORANDUM CULTURAL
CUBANO/BERMUDENSE

sabian.com

OPEN AND CLOSE HI-HAT EXECUTION

The opening and closing of the Hi-Hat has become a very important and colourful effect in this style of drumming. This effect is created by the Hi-Hat foot, which moves in a heel toe, heel toe motion, to open the Hi-Hat. When played, the top cymbal is slightly touching the bottom cymbal to create this special effect. This requires good co-ordination : work on it, until you are certain that it is being played to perfection.

PRACTICE EXAMPLES GIVEN :

Example 1 : Open Hi-Hat

Heel down on the count of 1.   Toe up, to open.

Example 2 : Hi-Hat Close

Toe down, heel up, to close.

Example 3 : Written

NOTE : Only when playing the Hi-Hat, when indicated, accentuate the Hi-Hat eighth notes.

Example : Accentuate Down beats on Hi-Hat.

Example : Accentuate Upbeats on Hi-Hat.

50

APERTURA Y CIERRE DE EJECUCIÓN HI-HAT

La apertura y cierre del Hi-Hat se ha convertido en un efecto muy importante y colorido en este estilo de tocar la batería. Este efecto se crea por el pie de Hi-Hat que se mueve en un dedo del pie del talón, el movimiento del dedo del pie talón, para abrir el Hi-Hat. Cuando se juega, el platillo superior está ligeramente tocar el platillo de fondo para crear este efecto especial. Esto requiere una buena coordinación : que trabajen en ella, hasta que esté seguro que se está jugando a la perfección.

EJEMPLOS DETERMINADA PRÁCTICA :

Ejemplo 1 : Hi-Hat (platillos) abiertos

Tálon hacia abajo en la cuenta de 1.   *Dedo del pie para arriba, para abrir.*

Ejemplo 2 : Hi-Hat Cerrados

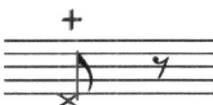

Coloque el pied hacia abajo y el talon hasta para cerrar.

Ejemplo 3 : Escrito

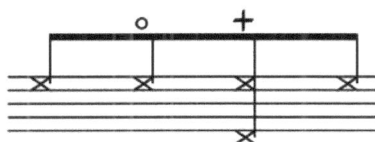

***NOTA**: Acentúan las notas corcheas de Hi-Hat Sólo cuando esté indicado.*

Ejemplo : Tocar el Hi-Hat (platillos cerrado) en el tiempo.

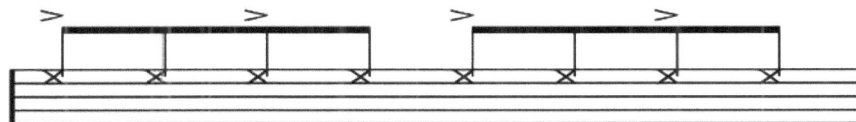

Ejemplo : Tocar el Hi-Hat a contratiempo.

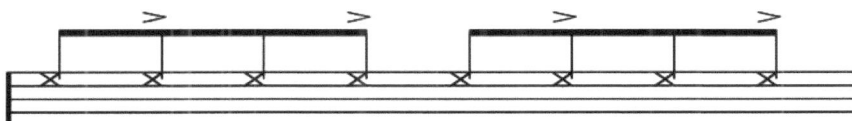

HI-HAT OFF BEATS

The two examples of measures given on this page, are designed to allow you to get familiar with eighth note Hi-Hat Off Beats.

Practice each example given individually, then, and only when you are comfortable, practice both measures together as one groove, and focus on the sound, and the feel, that you are creating with just the Hi-Hat alone.

Example A : 1 Bar Close Hi-Hat Off Beats.

Example B : 1 Bar Close and Open Hi-Hat Off Beats.

Examples A and B Combined as One Hi-Hat Groove.

As a reminder: This is not where it all stops. Continue to practice the examples given, and create your own one or two measure phrases.

CONTRATIEMPO DE HI-HAT

Los dos ejemplos de las medidas dadas en esta página, están diseñados para permitir que usted se familiarice con corcheas Hi-Hat en contratiempo.

Practica cada ejemplo dado por separado, entonces, y sólo cuando se sienta cómodo, la práctica ambas medidas como una sola ranura, y se centran en el sonido y las sensación de que va a crear sólo con el Hi-Hat solo.

Ejemplo A : 1 compás con Hi-Hat cerrado tocando contratiempo.

Ejemplo B : 1 compás cerrado y abierto tocando Hi-Hat contratiempo.

Ejemplos A y B combinados como un groove de Hi-Hat.

Como recordatorio: esto no es donde todo se detiene. Continuar con la práctica de los ejemplos dados, y crear su propio frases de uno o dos compases.

La Escuela Elemental de Música Alejandro García Caturla

Havana, CUBA

Presents its 2010

WORKSHOP SERIES

Conducted by Bermudian Professor Eddie Ming

Accompanied by Loidel Elías Hernández

Entitled:

PARADIDDLE JOHNNIE

Hosted by

Eddie Ming's

Drum School and Rhythm Lab

Bermuda

To be held on

Monday, 29th November 2010

At The Alejandro García Caturla Elementary School of Music

From 10.00 a.m. to 12.00 p.m.

For more information please call 'CATURLA' at 260-4525

Sponsored by

Eddie Ming's Drum School and Rhythm Lab, BERMUDA

La Escuela Elemental de Musica Alejandro Garcia Caturla

presenta su serie

TALLERES 2010

Conducido por

el Profesor Eddie Ming de Islas Bermudas

Acompanado por

Loidel Elías Hernández

Titulo

Rudimento (Paradiddle) Johnnie

Auspiciado por

LA ESCUELA DE LA BATERÍA

DE EDDIE MING

Y EL LABORATORIO DEL RITMO

Las Bermudas

Tendra lugar

el Lunes, 29 de Noviembre 2010

en la Escuela Alejandro Garcia Caturla

de 10:00 a.m. a 12:00 p.m.

Para más información, llamar a CATURLA al telefono 260 4525

Patrocinado por

La Escuela de la Batería de Eddie Ming y El Laboratorio del Ritmo,

Las Bermudas

The December 2010 workshop at 'CATURLA' was designed to orchestrate the basic single Paradiddle for the development of FUNK and FILLS.

FOR EXAMPLE :

Groove :

Fill-In :

Groove :

Fill-In :

The combinations are endless.

El taller en diciembre 2010 "Caturla" fue diseñado para orquestar la base Paradiddle único para el desarrollo de Funk y Rellenos.

OR EJEMPLO :

Groove :

Relleno :

Groove :

Relleno :

Las combinaciones son infinitas.

Dedicated to Victor Lino Rodríguez

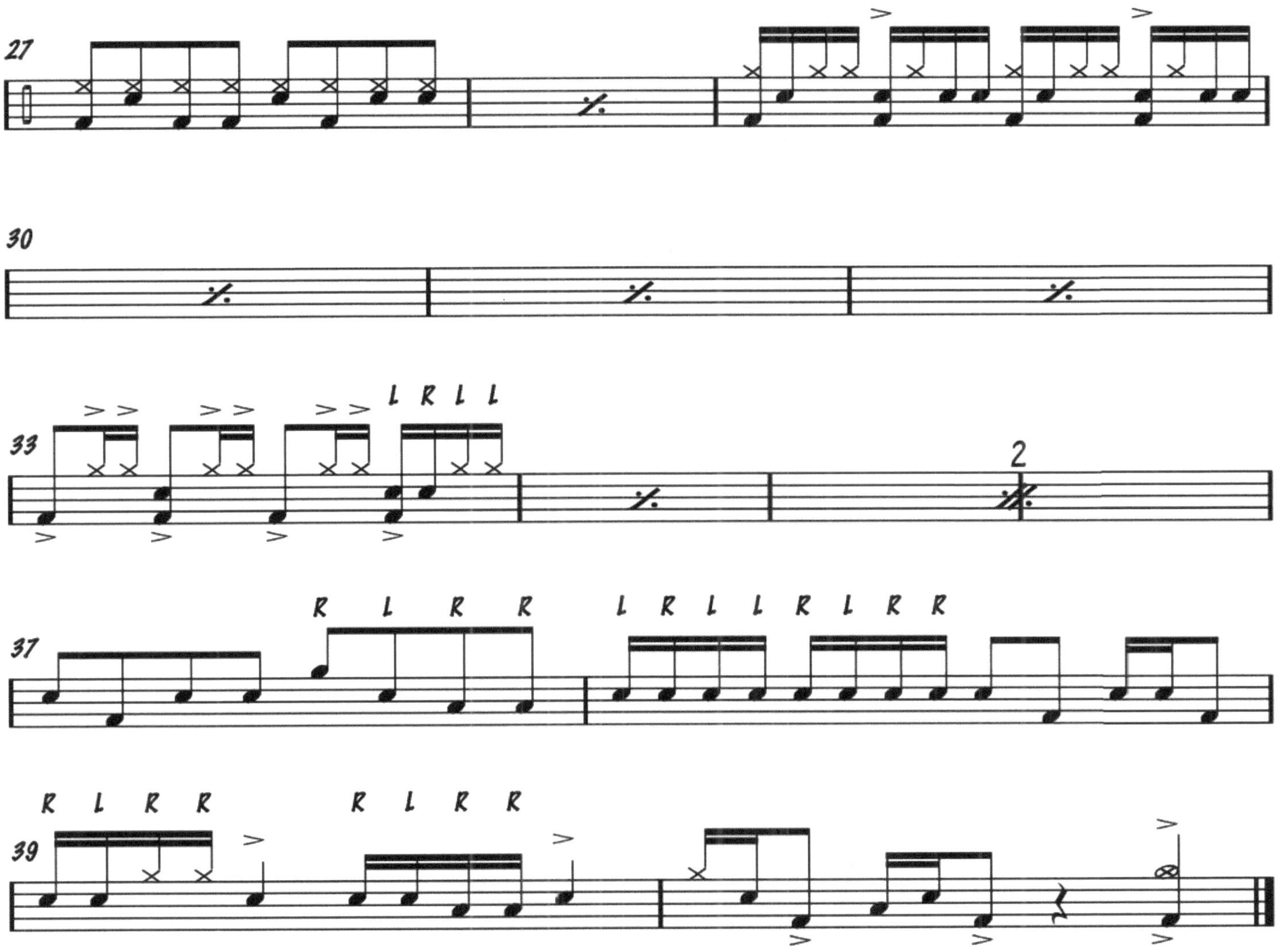
27
30
33
L R L L
2
37
R L R R
L R L L R L R R
39
R L R R
R L R R

Dedicated to Angel Ruiz Mora

R L R R L R L L R L
26
R L R R
28
31
R L R R L L
33
R L R R
36
R L R R L R L L R L R R L L L
40

Dedicated to William Vázquez Figueroa

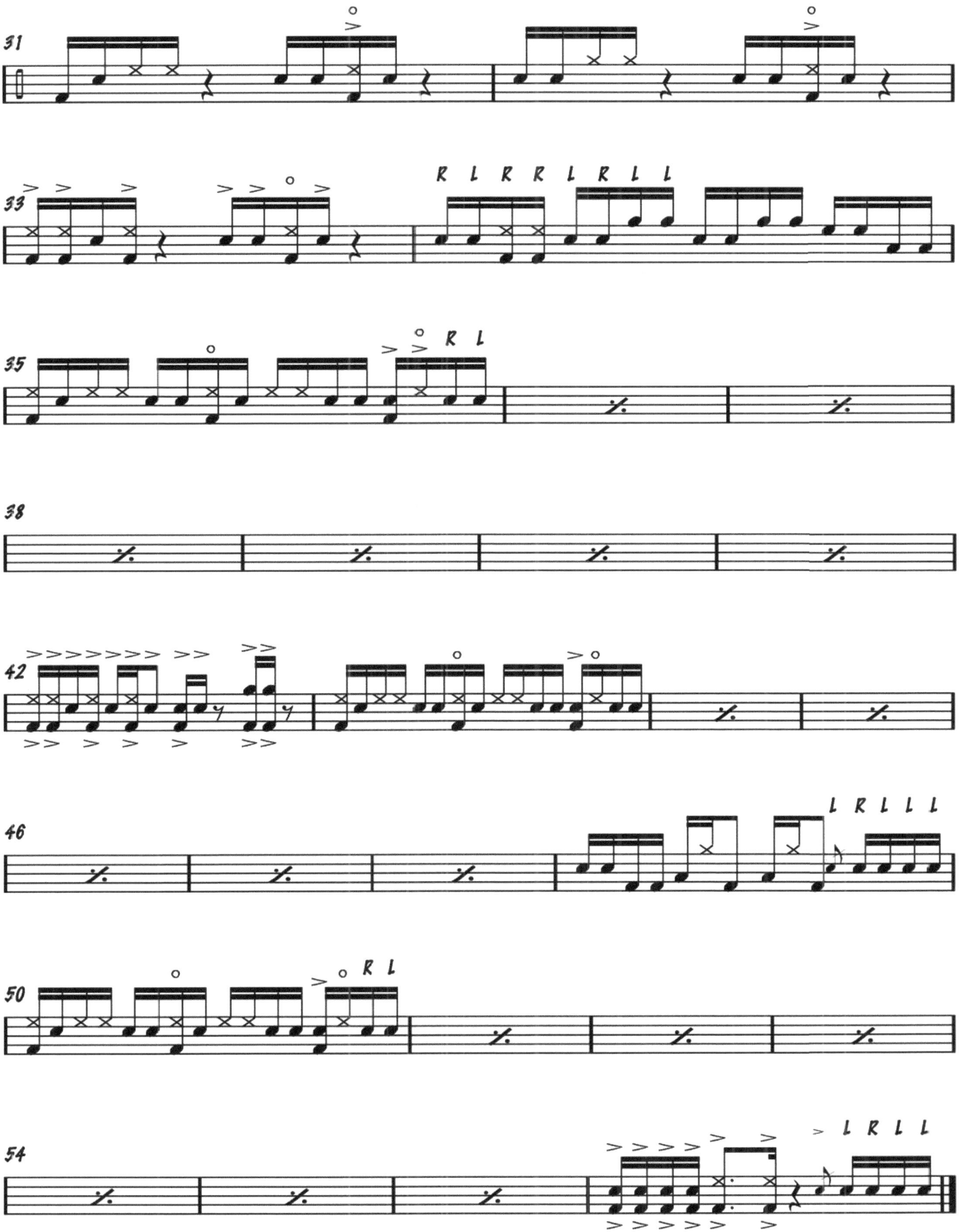
31
33
R L R R L R L L
35
R L
38
42
46
L R L L L
50
R L
54
L R L L

Dedicated to Edgar Alvarez Rodríguez

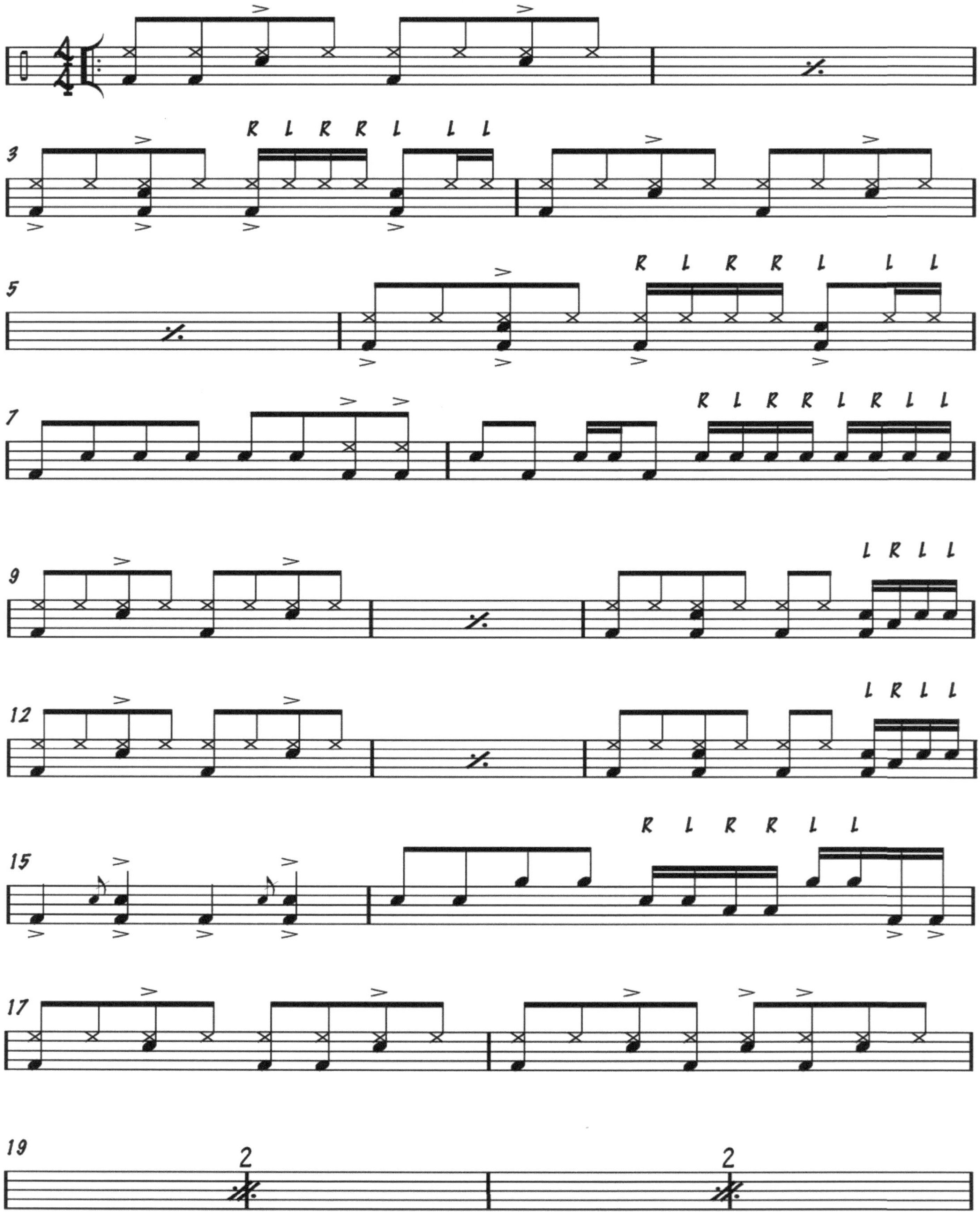

23
R L R R R L R R
R L R R L L R L R R
25
27
2
R L R R L R L L
31
R L R R L R L L
R L R R L R L L R L R R L R L L

Dedicated to Victor Pérez Aldana

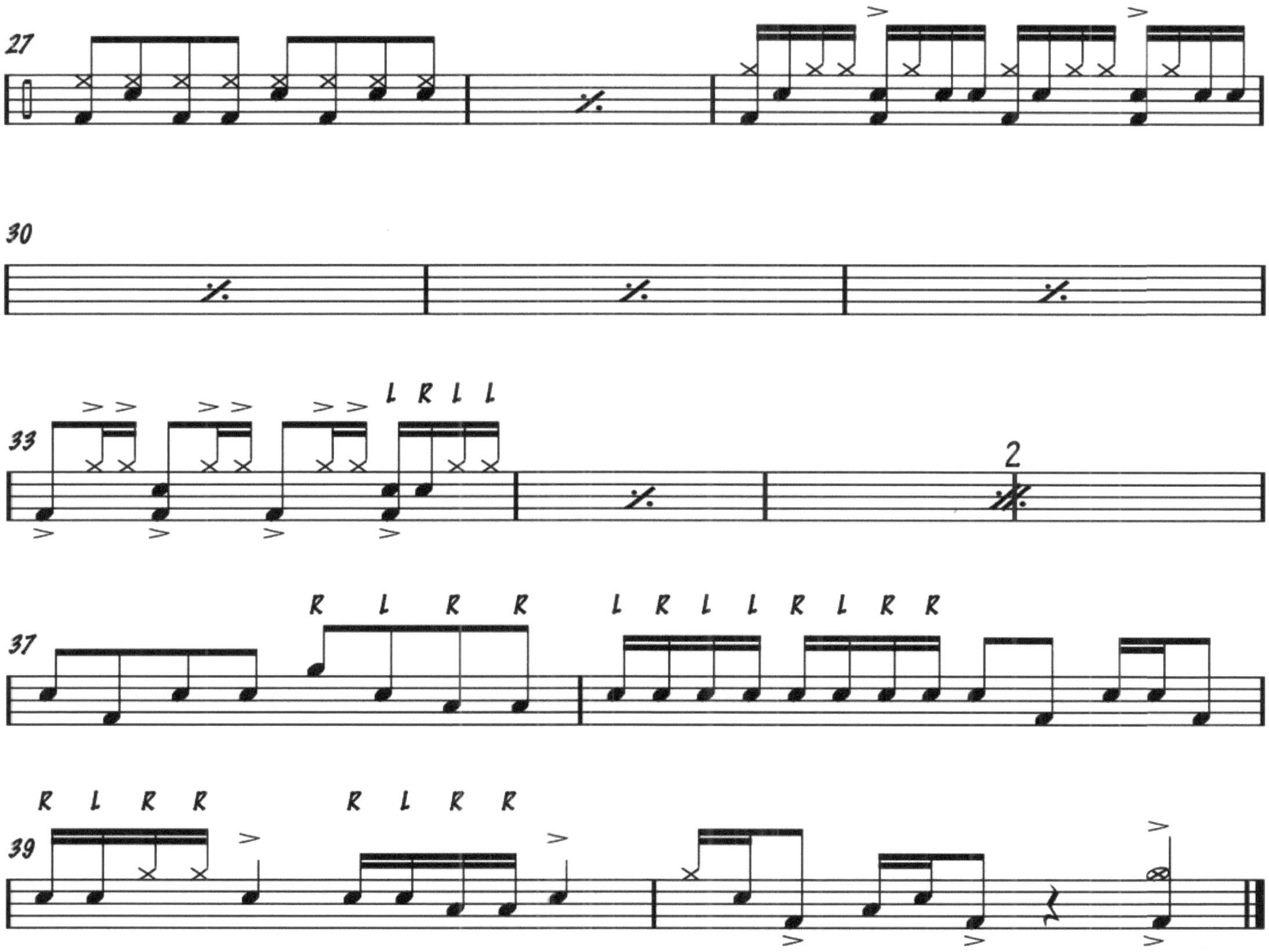
27
30
33
L R L L
2
37
R L R R
L R L L R L R R
39
R L R R
R L R R

Dedicated Amalia Salas Fernández

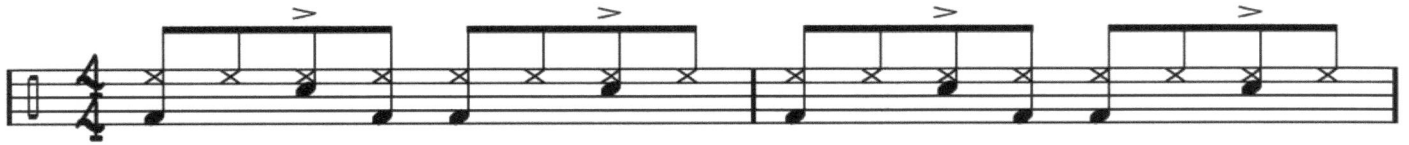

R L R R R L R R L R L L R L R L R L R R L R L L
21
23
25
27
R L R R L R L L R L R R L R L L L R L L
29

Dedicated To Elianet Pérez Lau

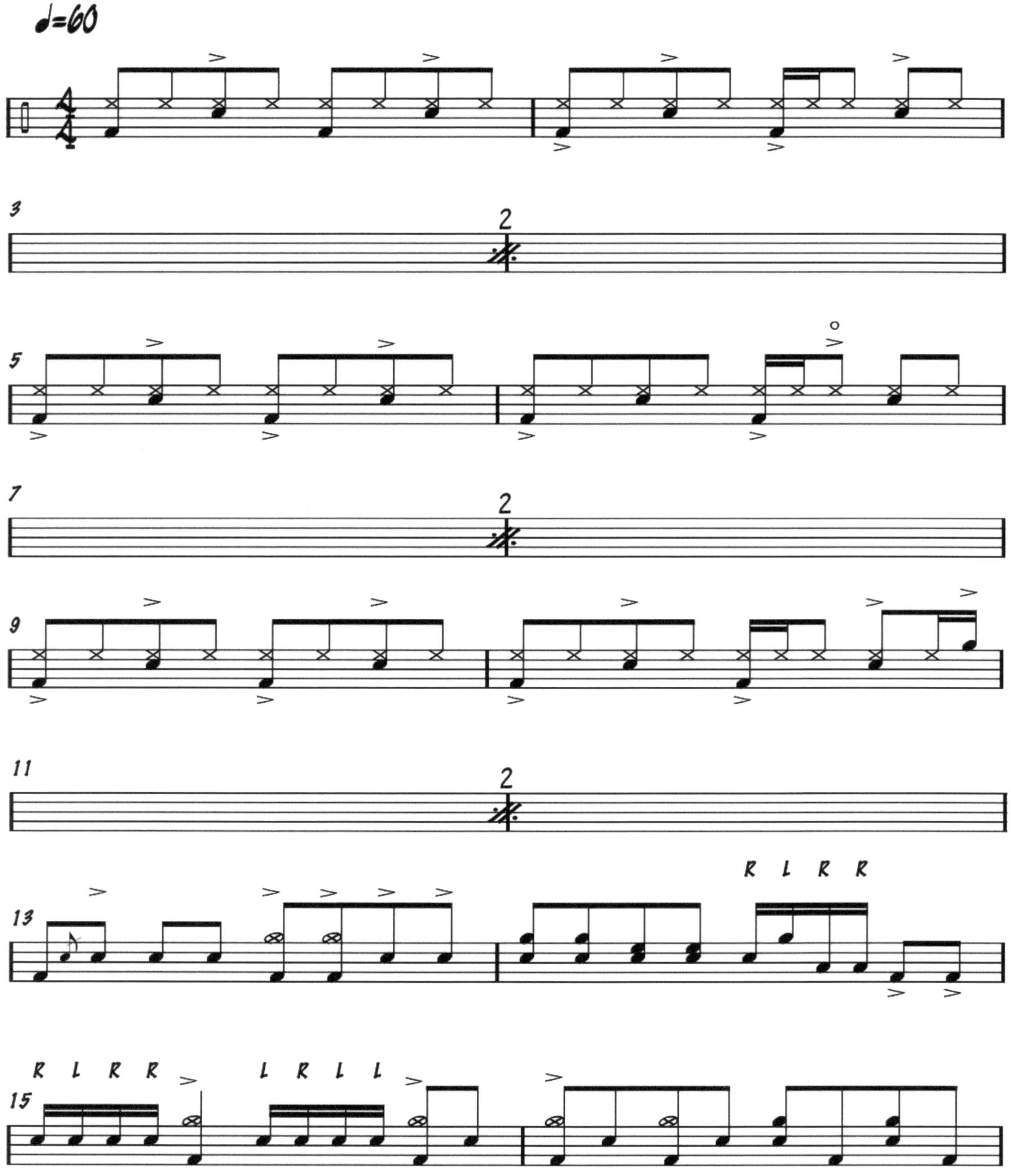

17
19
2
21
L R L L L R L L R R L R R L R L R R L R L L
23
25
27
2
29
R L R R L R L L R L L R R L R R L R R
31

Dedicated To Reynaldo Morales P

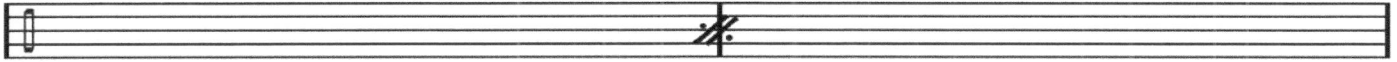

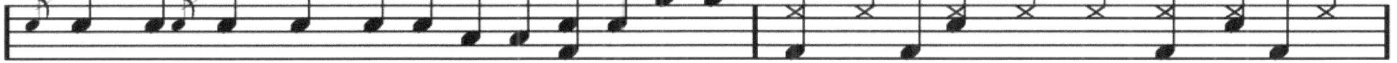

Dedicated To Andrés Desvergnine Arias

Dedicated To Loidel Elías Hernández

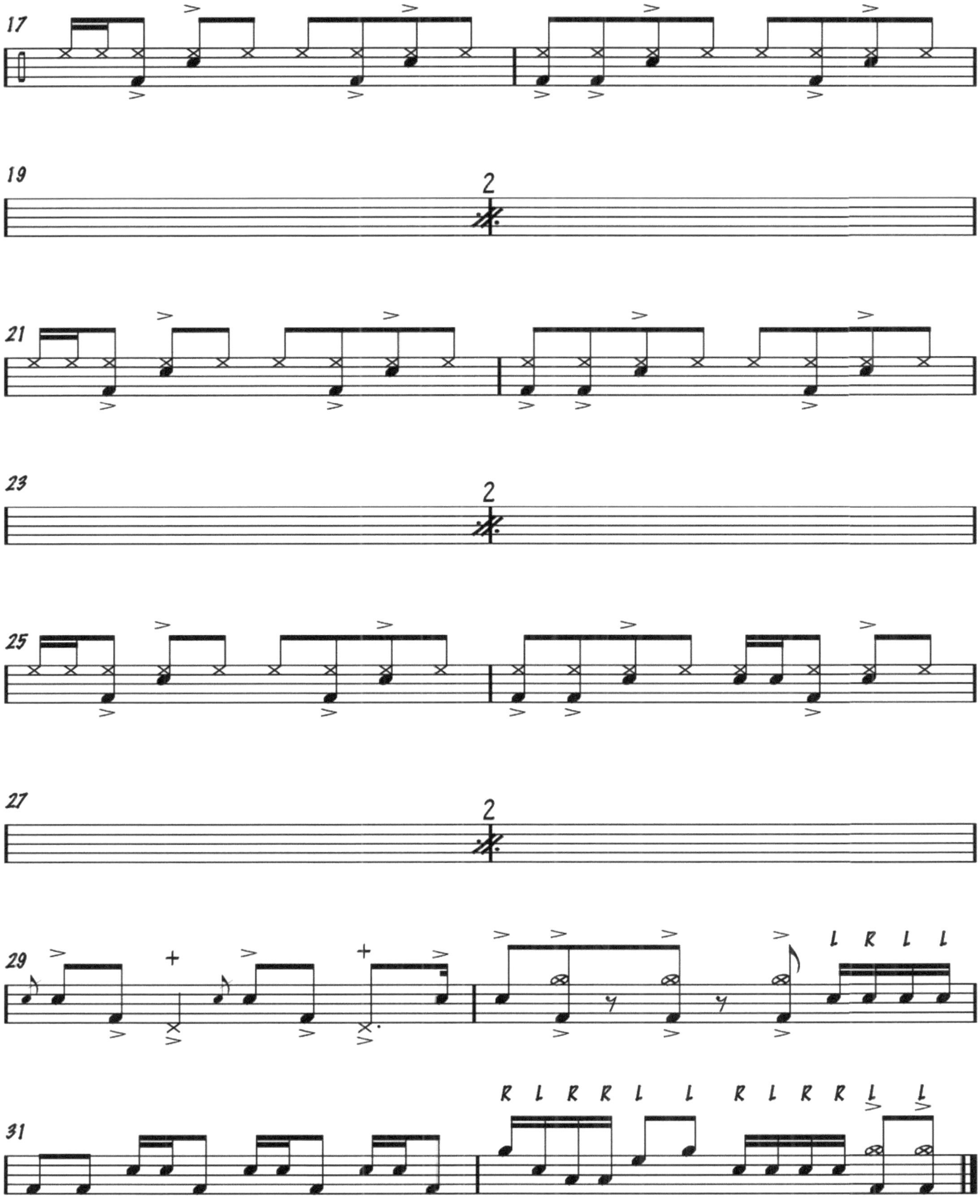
17
19
2
21
23
2
25
27
2
29
+
+
L R L L
31
R L R R L L R L R R L L

BIOGRAPHY OF ALEJANDRO GARCIA CATURLA

after whom The Alejandro Garcia Caturla Elementary Music School was named.

Alejandro Garcia Caturla (born on March 7, 1906 and died on November 12, 1940), was a Cuban composer of art music and creolized Cuban themes. He was born in Remedios. At the age of sixteen, he became a second violin of the new 'Orquesta Sinfonica de La Habana' in 1922, where Amadeo Roldan was concert-master (first-chair violin). Caturla also began composing at a young age, whilst studying both music and law. He was fascinated by creolized Afro-Cuban rhythms and these creole themes were characteristic of his compositions : the division between art music and popular music did not influence Cuban composers of this period.

After his student days, Caturla lived all of his life in the small central town of Remedios, where he became a lawyer to support his growing family. His 'Tres Danzas Cubanas' for symphony orchestra was first performed in Spain in 1929. 'Bembe' was premiered in Havana the same year. In 1932, he founded the Caibarien Concert Society, whose orchestra he conducted on many occasions. His 'Obertura Cubana' won first prize in a national contest in 1938. He was also a multi-instrumental musical performer and a baritone singer of some quality. Caturla was a fine man, and an example of a universal musician, happily combining classical and folkloric themes with modern musical ideas. He was murdered at the age of 34 by a young gambler who was due to be sentenced only hours later.

Alejandro Garcia Caturla's career followed a similar path to Amadeo Roldan, and the two men are considered to be pioneers of modern Cuban symphonic art.

BIOGRAFÍA DE ALEJANDRO GARCIA CATURLA

después de que La Escuela Elemental de Música 'Alejandro García Caturla' fue nombrado.

Nace: 07 de marzo de 1907 en Remedios, actual provincial de Villa Clara, Cuba. Muere: 12 de noviembre de 1940. Realizó los primeros studios musicales con Fernando Estrems y posteriormente con María Montalván y Carmen Valdés. Al pasar a La Habana para cursar estudios de Derecho en la Universidad (1922) estudió con Pedro Sanjuán Nortes armonía, contrapunto y fuga. En junio de 1928 marchó a París. Allí estudió con Nadia Boulanger. Este viaje fue consecuencia de su relación con Alejo Carpentier y otros miembros del Grupo Minorista. A su regreso a Cuba continuó desarollandose como compositor, compartiendo estas tareas con el ejercicio de su profesión. En septiembre de 1929 viajó de nuevo a Europa para representar a nuestro país junto a Eduardo Sánchez de Fuentes en los Festivales Sinfónicos Iberoamericanos de la Exposición Internacional de Barcelona, donde se ejecutó 'Tres Danzas Cubanas' para Orquesta Sinfónica En 1932 funda la Sociedad de Conciertos de Caibarién, de cuya orquesta fue director. En 1938, ganó el primer premio con 'Obertura Cubana,' en el Concurso Nacional de Música convocado en 1937 por la Dirección de Cultura de la Secretaría de Educación y Mención Honorífica por 'Suite para Orquesta.' A través de su corta vida desarrolló múltiples actividades como violinista, ocupó atriles de segundo violín y viola en la Orquesta Sinfónica de La Habana y la Filarmónica. Como pianista se inició tocando en un jazz band del cual fue director haciendo algunas presentaciones personales, además tocaba saxofón, clarinete y percusión. Su voz de baritono se escuchó en algunos conciertos organizados por Annkerman y Lecuona. Cultivó el periodismo como cronista social y crítico de arte, dejó trabajos sobre pedagogía musical y sobre la música nueva de su momento. Su preocupación por la justicia lo llevó a realizar importantes trabajos entre los que se encuentra un ensayo sobre la delincuencia juvenil. Ejerció jurídicamente en varios municipios, manteniendo una conducta intransigente en el ejercicio de su profesión. Su carácter, en permanente lucha con los convencionalismos sociales y artísticos lo llevo a la muerte.

La carrera de Alejandro García Caturla seguido una trayectoria similar a Amadeo Roldán, y los dos hombres son considerados pioneros del arte modern sinfónica cubana.

Ming and Daylí Santa Clara,

just before his December 18, 2010 Workshop Recital, which was held at

Cuba's Cine Teatro Avenida.

Daylí is a member of Ming's 10 Member Workshop Ensemble.

Eddie and his "Caturla" drum students (2010)

APPRECIATION

I would like to express my appreciation to all of my students at Cuba's Escuela Elemental De Música 'Alejandro Garcia Caturla', who motivated me into creating this drum book. I thought that by having this text, it would make it possible for all of the elementary students at 'Caturla' to be the first in all of Cuba, to have an in depth understanding for this style of drumming. In the years to come, it is my hope and wish that all of you students will become highly respected for your ability to play and teach, and that you will pass this information on to the next generation.

Listed below, are the names of the 10 Percussion students that I had the opportunity of teaching at 'CATURLA' in December 2009:

Angel Ruiz Mora

Andrés Desvergnine Arias

Victor Pérez Aldana

Loidel Elías Hernández

Reinaldo Morales P.

Edgar Alvarez Rodríguez

Elianet Pérez Lau

Amalia Salas Fernández

Victor Lino Rodríguez

William Vázquez Figueroa

To all the students listed above:

Please find your name highlighted on one of the last ten pages in this text book.

Finally,

I wish to give the glory to God,

because without Him,

nothing is possible.

Eddie Ming

2010

LA APRECIACIÓN

Querría expresar mi apreciación a todos mis estudiantes en la Escuela Elemental de Música 'Alejandro Garcia Caturla' de Cuba, que me motivó a crear este libro de batería. Pensé que teniendo este texto, lo haría posible para todos los alumnos de primaria en 'Caturla' para ser el primer en toda la Cuba, para tener una comprensión en profundidad para este estilo de golpetear. En los años para venir, es mi esperanza y el deseo que todos ustedes estudiantes llegarán a ser sumamente respetados para su capacidad de jugar y enseñar; y que pasará esta información en a la próxima generación.

Listó abajo, sean los nombres de los diez estudiantes de Percusión que tuve la oportunidad de enseñar en 'Caturla' en diciembre 2009.

Angel Ruiz Mora

Andrés Desvergnine Arias

Victor Pérez Aldana

Loidel Elías Hernández

Reinaldo Morales P.

Edgar Alvarez Rodríguez

Elianet Pérez Lau

Amalia Salas Fernández

Victor Lino Rodríguez

William Vázquez Figueroa

A todos los estudiantes listó arriba: Encuentre por favor su nombre destacado en uno de las últimas diez páginas en este libro de texto.

Por último,

yo deseo dar la gloria a Dios,

porque sin El,

nada es possible.

Eddie Ming

2010

February 2, 2010

Eddie Ming's Drum School &
Rhythm Lab
9 -39 Cut Road
St. George's GE 04
Bermuda

Attention: Professor Eddie Ming

Dear Eddie:

We at SABIAN wish to congratulate you on your new diploma and all the fine work you've done for us and for music in Cuba.

Your fine work does indeed coincide with all our efforts to spread the value of music there.

Best Regards from us all,
SABIAN

Robert Zildjian

THE HISTORY OF SABIAN

Robert Zildjian, founder and director of SABIAN, has forty years of experience in cymbal making behind him. In January 1982, he introduced his new cymbal manufacturing company to the competitive world market, under a new name - S A B I A N, named after his children : Sally, Billy, and Andy (who are all involved with the company of SABIAN Cymbal Makers, in various managerial roles).

SABIAN is located in Meductic's Main Street, in southern New Brunswick, Canada, where hundreds of models in six different series are manufactured.

Robert (Bob) Zildjian is proud of SABIAN. He credits his employees with having built the company into a strong family business, with a positive worldwide image.

We at the Escuela Elemental de Música Alejandro Garcia Caturla, are very happy to have Bob and SABIAN as our sponsors here, in Havana, Cuba.

Prof. Eddie Ming

LA HISTORIA DE SABIAN

Roberto Zildjian, fundador y director de Sabian, tiene cuarenta años de experiencia en la fabricación de platillos detrás de él. En enero de 1982, presentó su nueva compañia de fabricación de platillos al mercado mundial competitive, bajo un nuevo nombre – SABIAN, el nombre de sus hijos: Sally, Billy, y Andy (que son todos los involucrados con la empresa de SABIAN fabricantes de platillos, en varios las funciones de dirección).

Sabian se encuentra en la calle principal del Meductic, en el sur de Nueva Brunswick, Canadá, donde cientos de modelos en seis series diferentes de fabricación.

Roberto Zildjian se siente orgullosa de SABIAN – él créditos a sus empleados por haber construido la empresa en un negocio familiar fuerte, con una imagen en todo el mundo positivo.

Nosotros en el Escuela Elemental de Música Alejandro García Caturla son muy felices de tener Bob y SABIAN como a nuestros patrocinadores que aquí, en La Habana, Cuba.

Prof. Eddie Ming

ACKNOWLEDGEMENTS

AGRADECIMIENTOS

Eddie wishes to thank the following people for their kind assistance with the Spanish translation of this text :

Eddie desea agradecer a las siguientes personas por su amable ayuda con la traducción al español de este texto :

Aldo Mazza

Profesor Sonia Salas

Profesor Alejandro Vázquez

Profesor Alexis Sánchez

Wendy Ming

Tanya Walker

Sylvia Rodríguez

El señor Vicente Pouso Martin

(Español)

Reseña del libro
"Batería Tradicional, Grooves Clásicos y Rellenos para Recitales del Laboratorio de Ritmos"
del autor y profesor bermudeño Eddie Ming,

por Agustin Gómez Lavín, *professor de percusión del Conservatorio "Amadeo Roldán y el Instituto Superior de Arte, Havana, Cuba.*

La extensa práctica como profesor e intéprete del maestro Eddie Ming brinda a los estudiantes de percusión la noción de patrones y ritmos internacionales de forma eficaz, musical y didáctica. El libro abarca piezas de los ritmos Funk, Rock, y Rhythm and Blues que contribuyen eficazmente al aprendizaje de estos ritmos internacionales. Esto constituye un desafío para los estudiantes cubanos por la posibilidad que les ofrece de ponerse en contacto con nuevos estilos musicales. Este libro contiene material extra interesante que amplía y profundiza en la aplicación de la batería tradicional en los propios grooves y rellenos que ofrece. Por tales razones, es un valioso libro de consulta para estudiantes y profesores de percusión.

(English)

Book Review of Bermudian author and professor, Eddie Ming's
"The Rhythm Lab's Traditional Drum Set Classic Grooves and Fills For Recitals"
by Agustin Gómez Lavín, professor of percussion at the Conservatory "Amadeo Roldán," and the University For The Arts, Havana, Cuba.

With an enormous amount of experience behind him, professor and musician, Eddie Ming, presents percussion students with an understanding of international patterns and rhythms in an efficient, musical and instructive way, which contributes to their comprehensive learning. This book covers *Funk, Rock, and Rhythm and Blues,* and is a challenge for Cuban students, for the possibility that it offers them to get in contact with new musical styles. The book contains an interesting bonus material, which widens and goes deeper into the application of the traditional drum set in the very same grooves and fills that it provides. For all these reasons, this is a valuable book to be consulted and used by percussion students and teachers.

Music Schools in Cuba
where Bermudian author & professor,
EDDIE MING, has taught:-

Escuela Elemental de Música, "Alejandro García Caturla"
The Alejandro García Caturla Elementary School of Music

Escuela Elemental de Música "Manuel Saumell"
The Manuel Saumell Elementary Music Academy

Escuela Elemental y Conservatorio de Música "Guillermo Tomás"
The Guillermo Tomás Elementary School and Conservatory of Music

Escuela Nacional de Música
The National School of Music of Cuba

Conservatorio "Amadeo Roldán
The Amadeo Roldán Conservatory

Conservatorio "Carlos Hidalgo Díaz"
The Carlos Hidalgo Díaz Conservatory

Escuela Vocacional de Arte "Pedro Raúl Sánchez"
The Pedro Raúl Sánchez Vocational School of Art

Escuela Provincial de Arte "Eduardo Abela Villareal"
The Eduardo Abela Villareal Provincial School of Art

ISA
The University of Arts of Cuba

Escuela Vocacional de Arte "Alfonso Pérez Isaac"
The Alfonso Pérez Isaac Vocational School of Art

Escuela Elemental de Música "Paulita Concepción"
The Paulita Concepción Elementary School of Music

Introducing
Three RHYTHM LAB Books For Drum Set
by Eddie Ming

ISBN 9781535325844

ISBN 978-0-9569878-1-5

ISBN 9781519238269

ARTISTIC ORCHESTRATED APPLICATIONS FOR DRUM SET

For the intermediate student, and also for teachers who want to enhance their creative skills.

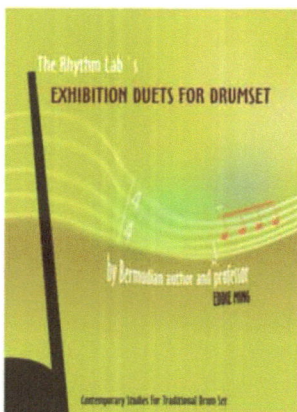

EXHIBITION DUETS FOR DRUM SET

This book provides 38 Bonus Solo Ideas and 6/8 Bonus Grooves that should be explored. For the intermediate performer.

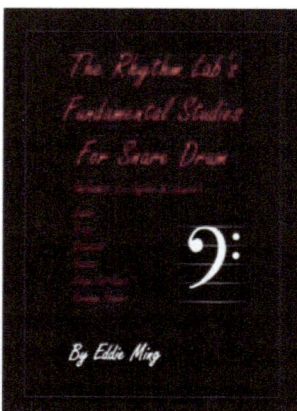

FUNDAMENTAL STUDIES FOR SNARE DRUM

For the young ones who are enthusiastic about developing their reading skills.

Presentando
Tres Libres Para Batería
Del LABORATORIO DE RITMO
por Eddie Ming

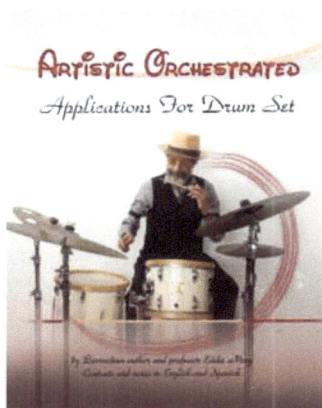

ISBN 9781535325844

APLICACIONES ARTÍSTICAS ORQUESTADAS PARA BATERÍA

Para el estudiante de nivel medio y también para profesores que quieran mejorar sus habilidades creativas.

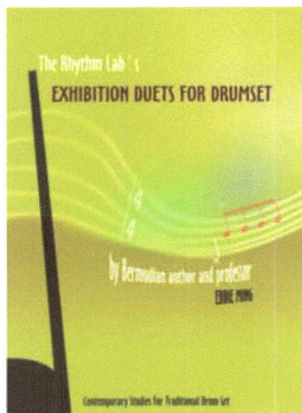

ISBN 978-0-9569878-1-5

DÚOS DE EXHIBICIÓN PARA BATERÍA

Este libro está provisto de 38 ideas extras para solos y patrones en 6/8 que deben ser examinados. Para el intérprete de nivel medio.

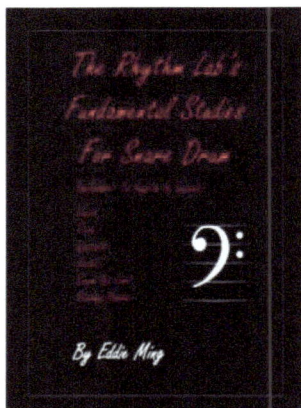

ISBN 9781519238269

ESTUDIOS FUNDAMENTALES DE CAJA

Para los jóvenes que están muy entusiasmados con el desarollo de sus habilidades de lectura.

www.ingramcontent.com/pod-product-compliance
Lightning Source LLC
Chambersburg PA
CBHW042009080426
42734CB00002B/26